One Little, Two Little, Three Little Pilgrims

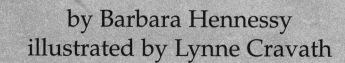

by Barbara Hennessy
illustrated by Lynne Cravath

SCHOLASTIC INC.
New York Toronto London Auckland Sydney
Mexico City New Delhi Hong Kong

ISBN 0-439-23206-6

Text copyright © 1999 by B.G. Hennessy. Illustrations copyright © 1999 by Lynne Cravath.
All rights reserved. Published by Scholastic Inc., 555 Broadway, New York, NY 10012,
by arrangement with Viking, a division of Penguin Putnam Books for Young Readers.
SCHOLASTIC and associated logos are trademarks
and/or registered trademarks of Scholastic Inc.

12 11 10 9 8 7 6 5 4 3 2 1   0 1 2 3 4 5/0

Printed in the U.S.A.   08

First Scholastic printing, November 2000
Set in Palatino

For Devon and Sarah
—B. H.

For Carrie, with love
—L. C.

1 little,

2 little,

3 little Pilgrims.

4 little, 5 little, 6 little Pilgrims.

7 little, 8 little, 9 little Pilgrims.

10 little Pilgrim boys and girls.

1 little,

2 little, 3 little Wampanoag.

4 little,

5 little,

6 little Wampanoag.

7 little, 8 little, 9 little Wampanoag.

10 little Wampanoag boys and girls.

Digging for clams. Fishing for cod.

Hunting for ducks, rabbits, and geese.

Planting crops of corn and beans.

Everyone has a job to do.

Digging for turnips, carrots, and beets.

Gathering nuts, berries, and squash.

Carrying baskets of barley and corn.

Now it's time to celebrate!

1 big,

2 big,

3 big turkeys.

4 big, 5 big, 6 big turkeys.

7 big, 8 big, 9 big turkeys.

10 big turkeys for the feast.

Turkey, cornbread, cranberry stuffing.
Pumpkin, cider, Indian pudding.
Clams and oysters—tummies growling.

Let's give thanks and then we'll eat!

A Note from the Author

Is this book about the first Thanksgiving?

No. It is meant to give a general picture of Pilgrim and Wampanoag life. The three day feast that we know as "The First Thanksgiving" was held in Plimoth (now Plymouth) in 1621 to celebrate the harvest.

Who are the Wampanoag?

Wampanoag (Wam-pa-NO-ag) means "People of the Dawn." Cape Cod is one of the easternmost points in North America; that's where the sun rises first in the morning. The Wampanoag belong to the Algonquin-speaking peoples.

Did the children really work this hard?

Yes, they did. Everyone worked hard. The Wampanoag people often worked in family groups. Sometimes the entire family would hunt or fish. During the harsh winters the men and boys would go off to hunt while the women and girls took care of the home.

Why is the Wampanoag boy planting a fish?

He certainly doesn't expect it to grow! When seeds were planted a dead fish was put in the same mound. As the fish rotted it provided nutrients for the plants, like a private compost pile. This was one of the most useful things the Wampanoag taught the Pilgrims.

Fish for a harvest feast?

Yes, oysters, lobster, clams, cod, herring, salmon, and eels. Plimoth is located just north of Cape Cod in New England. It was one of the richest fishing areas in the world. But when the colonists first arrived they did not know the best ways to fish. Squanto, an adopted member of the Wampanoag village, taught the

Pilgrims many fishing and planting techniques. These techniques were very important in helping the Pilgrims survive.

Where's the popcorn? What about the pumpkin pie?

It is true that corn was a staple part of the Wampanoag diet and an ingredient in many recipes, but it is unlikely that popcorn as we know it was part of a Wampanoag feast. Popcorn was introduced to this area in the late 1700s. Sugar, or any kind of sweetener, would have been rare in Plimoth. There were very few desserts. People did eat "pudding" type dishes that were made with corn and berries and perhaps honey or maple syrup.

O. K., they did have turkey.

They also ate other wild birds, ducks and geese, as well as deer meat, called venison.

Did they really give "thanks"?

Yes, they did. A prayer of thanks to God was a routine part of Pilgrim life, and the Wampanoag had five traditional thanksgiving festivals every year, and certainly offered thanks to a higher power for their survival.

A Note from the Illustrator

It was a pleasant surprise to find out how much information exists about everyday life so long ago. Through books and with the help of the research director of Plimoth Plantation, I found material about the clothes, table manners, dishes, utensils, and dwellings of the Pilgrims. There were many detailed pictures of Wampanoag life: clothing, hairstyles, canoes, dwellings, fishing and hunting methods. After assembling all that information, I enjoyed imagining and creating this happy harvest celebration.

Bibliography

Anderson, Joan. *The First Thanksgiving Feast*. Photographs by George Ancona. New York: Clarion, 1984.

Loeb, Robert H. *Meet the Real Pilgrims: Everyday Life in Plimoth Plantation in 1627*. Garden City, New York: Doubleday, 1979.

Peters, Russell M. *Clambake: A Wampanoag Tradition*. Photographs by John Madama. Minneapolis: Lerner Publications, 1992.

Peters, Russell M. *The Wampanoag of Mashpee*. Boston: Nimrod Press, Indian Spiritual and Cultural Training Council, 1987.

Sewall, Marcia. *The Pilgrims of Plimoth*. New York: Atheneum, 1986.

Travers, Milton A. *The Wampanoag Indian Federation of the Algonquin Nation: Indian Neighbors of the Pilgrims*.   New Bedford, Massachusetts: Reynolds De Watt, 1957.

Waters, Kate. *Sarah Morton's Day: A Day in the Life of a Pilgrim Girl*. Photographs by Russell Kendall. New York: Scholastic, 1989.

Waters, Kate. *Tapenum's Day: A Wampanoag Indian Boy in Pilgrim Times*. Photographs by Russell Kendall. New York: Scholastic, 1966.

Weinstein-Farson, Laurie. *The Wampanoag*. New York: Chelsea House, 1989.

Wilbur, C. Keith. *The New England Indians*. Chester, Connecticut: Globe Pequot Press, 1978.

Web site for Plimoth Plantation: www.plimoth.org